Who W
Jim Hen

Who Was
Jim Henson?

By Joan Holub

Illustrated by Nancy Harrison

Grosset & Dunlap

An Imprint of Penguin Group (USA) Inc.

For Lorie Ann Grover—J.H.

GROSSET & DUNLAP
Published by the Penguin Group
Penguin Group (USA) Inc., 375 Hudson Street, New York, New York 10014, USA
Penguin Group (Canada), 90 Eglinton Avenue East, Suite 700,
Toronto, Ontario M4P 2Y3, Canada
(a division of Pearson Penguin Canada Inc.)
Penguin Books Ltd., 80 Strand, London WC2R 0RL, England
Penguin Group Ireland, 25 St. Stephen's Green, Dublin 2, Ireland
(a division of Penguin Books Ltd.)
Penguin Group (Australia), 250 Camberwell Road, Camberwell, Victoria 3124, Australia
(a division of Pearson Australia Group Pty. Ltd.)
Penguin Books India Pvt. Ltd., 11 Community Centre,
Panchsheel Park, New Delhi—110 017, India
Penguin Group (NZ), 67 Apollo Drive, Rosedale, North Shore 0632, New Zealand
(a division of Pearson New Zealand Ltd.)
Penguin Books (South Africa) (Pty.) Ltd., 24 Sturdee Avenue,
Rosebank, Johannesburg 2196, South Africa

Penguin Books Ltd., Registered Offices:
80 Strand, London WC2R 0RL, England

Text copyright © 2010 by Joan Holub. Illustrations copyright © 2010 by Nancy Harrison.
All rights reserved. Published by Grosset & Dunlap, a division of Penguin Young Readers
Group, 345 Hudson Street, New York, New York 10014. GROSSET & DUNLAP is a
trademark of Penguin Group (USA) Inc. Printed in the U.S.A.

Library of Congress Control Number: 2009044186

ISBN 978-0-448-45406-1   10 9 8 7 6 5 4 3 2

Contents

Who Was
Jim Henson?

He was the man behind the Muppets. He was Kermit the Frog. He was Ernie of Sesame Street. But at first, puppets were just a way for him to break into television. That was what he really wanted to do.

Although he could be shy, he managed to land a job in TV as a teenager. In college he got his very own TV puppet show!

Until Jim Henson, hand puppets and marionettes with strings were the main kinds of puppets. He invented a new kind. And he gave his puppets a new name—Muppets.

Jim was a tall, thin, soft-spoken guy. He looked gentle and serious—not silly. But from the start his Muppets were wild and silly. Today his Big

Bird, Miss Piggy, and Kermit the Frog are known around the world. He helped make *Sesame Street* one of the most popular children's shows ever.

Working hard made him happy. Jim wanted to make a difference in the world. And he did.

Chapter 1
Growing Up

Jim was born on September 24, 1936, in Greenville, Mississippi. His full name was James Maury Henson, but his family called him Jimmy. His brother, Paul, was two years older.

The boys grew up in Leland, near the Mississippi River. Leland was a small country town. To make a telephone call, you had to wind up the phone. You couldn't just dial a number.

Growing up there was fun. Down at the nearest creek, Jim and his brother went fishing and swimming with their cousins. They went

horseback riding and played tennis. Jim caught
turtles and frogs as pets. He was also a cub
scout and had a stamp collection. On Sundays,

the family often liked to play a game of croquet.

The Hensons were a happy family. They liked
to tell stories and joke around with each other.

Jim's mom, Betty, took care of the family and
house. She played the organ and the family
would sing along. His dad, who was also
named Paul, was a scientist working for the
US Department of Agriculture. He studied farm
crops, trying to find better ways to grow them.

His grandmother was nicknamed "Dear." She liked to paint, sew quilts, and she loved to read. Dear encouraged Jim's creativity and self-confidence. She was always ready to hear about whatever he was doing. Sometimes he would show his drawings of imaginary creatures to her.

They were monsters, but funny ones with curly beaks and stripes. After he became famous, people would ask who inspired him most. Jim Henson always said it was Dear.

In the 1930s and 1940s, families gathered in their living rooms to tune in to their favorite radio shows. After school, Jim liked to listen to *The Shadow*, a popular mystery show. *The Green Hornet* was a superhero show. A popular comedy show starred Edgar Bergen and a wooden puppet named Charlie McCarthy. These were all favorites of Jim's.

Then in the late 1940s and early 1950s something new came along and replaced radio: television.

Most families, including the Hensons, didn't own a television. In 1946, there were only 7,000 TVs in the whole country! The first popular kids' TV program didn't begin until Jim was eleven. It was *The Howdy Doody Show.*

When Jim was in fifth grade, his family moved. Their new home was in Hyattsville, Maryland, near Washington, D.C. Hyattsville was a lot bigger than Leland. Some people even had their own TVs.

Jim begged his parents to buy one. When he was about thirteen, they did. All the programs were in black-and-white. Color TVs weren't around yet. But Jim was hooked. When he was only sixteen, Jim went to nearby television stations asking for a job. He wanted to design sets, props, and scenery, but he would take any job. No one would hire him. He wasn't pushy, but he didn't like to take no for an answer.

By now, Jim and his brother were going to Northwestern High School. He got good grades, but art was his best subject. He drew cartoons for the school newspaper. Whenever he could, he illustrated his reports and projects.

In the summer before college, Jim heard exciting news. Local TV station WTOP needed puppeteers for a Saturday children's program called *The Junior Morning Show*. They were willing to hire students.

Jim wanted that job. The only problem was, he didn't know anything about puppetry. He'd never been to a live puppet show. But he had seen the popular TV puppet show called *Kukla, Fran and Ollie.*

He borrowed some library books about puppet making. At home in the kitchen, he and a friend made a few puppets out of his mom's fabric scraps. They created a French rat named Pierre,

who wore a beret. The idea for Pierre came from
one of the cartoons he'd drawn for his high
school paper. They also made cowboy puppets

named Longhorn and Shorthorn. Jim and his friend took them to the TV station. They got the job!

CHARLIE MCCARTHY

EDGAR BERGEN WAS A POPULAR VENTRILOQUIST. VENTRILOQUISTS ARE PEOPLE WHO CAN "THROW THEIR VOICES." WHEN EDGAR SPOKE, HE TRIED TO MAKE IT SEEM THAT HIS WORDS CAME FROM CHARLIE MCCARTHY. CHARLIE, A WOODEN DUMMY, SAT ON BERGEN'S KNEE. HE WORE A TOP HAT, SATIN CAPE, AND MONOCLE, AND WAS THE SIZE OF A SMALL BOY. THEIR RADIO SHOW BEGAN IN 1936. IT WAS SNAPPY AND FUNNY AND A HUGE HIT. CHARLIE WAS A BRATTY CHILD WHO HAD A FRESH ANSWER FOR EVERYTHING. WHEN TV BECAME BIG, EDGAR AND CHARLIE APPEARED ON SEVERAL SHOWS. BUT THEY NEVER HAD A SERIES OF THEIR OWN. JIM ADMIRED EDGAR BERGEN SO MUCH THAT HE DEDICATED HIS FIRST MOVIE (*THE MUPPET MOVIE*) TO HIM. BERGEN'S ONLY DAUGHTER IS ACTRESS CANDICE BERGEN.

KUKLA, FRAN AND OLLIE

BESIDES *HOWDY DOODY*, *KUKLA, FRAN AND OLLIE* WAS ANOTHER POPULAR CHILDREN'S SHOW IN THE EARLY DAYS OF TELEVISION. KUKLA AND OLLIE WERE HAND PUPPETS MADE BY PUPPETEER BURR TILLSTROM. KUKLA WAS A CLOWNLIKE BOY WITH A ROUND NOSE. OLLIE WAS A DRAGON WITH ONLY ONE TOOTH. THEY PERFORMED IN A SMALL BOXLIKE PUPPET THEATER WITH A STAGE. AN ACTRESS NAMED FRAN ALLISON CHATTED WITH THEM. FROM BEHIND THE STAGE, BURR OPERATED THE PUPPETS AND SPOKE FOR THEM. THE SHOW FIRST CAME ON TV IN 1947 AND WAS A BIG SUCCESS. VIEWERS CARED ABOUT KUKLA AND OLLIE AS IF THEY WERE REAL PEOPLE. AFTER KUKLA MADE OLLIE GO BALD IN ONE SHOW, FANS MAILED WIGS TO OLLIE. ONE BOY EVEN SENT GRASS SEED SINCE OLLIE WAS GREEN. THE SHOW RAN UNTIL 1957.

Chapter 2
The First Muppets

The Junior Morning Show only lasted a few weeks. But people had liked Jim's rat and cowboy puppets. He took them to WRC-TV, a local NBC station. They gave him little puppetry jobs here and there. But could he earn a living doing this? It didn't seem so.

After high school, Jim went to the University of Maryland to study art. He hoped to be a commercial artist.

class assignment:

He also took a puppetry class. Jim still didn't plan to make a career working with puppets. But in 1955 at the end of his freshman year, he got a huge break. Someone at WRC—probably the program director, but no one can recall for sure—decided to give him his own puppet show! He named it *Sam and Friends*. It came on for five minutes, twice a night, after the news. He earned five dollars a show. Sam was a funny-looking bald man with big ears made of carved plastiline covered with plastic wood. His friends included a purple skull-creature named Yorick.

Jim didn't know much about creating a TV show. That was okay. He got to figure out the best way to do things as he went along. He liked that.

Right away he decided to get rid of the boxlike puppet theater. For live shows, puppets always performed in a small stage. Hand puppeteers could hide in the side and bottom part of the stage to work their puppets. The marionette puppeteers could work theirs from above, often hidden behind a drape.

But on TV, a boxy stage framed inside a boxy TV screen didn't look very interesting. And on

TV, a boxy stage wasn't necessary. The TV screen itself was like a stage. Puppeteers could work outside the range of the TV camera and be "hidden" from viewers. So Jim set his puppets free. They did skits in front of painted backdrops. Sometimes they just danced all around the screen.

Jim worked all the puppets. He stayed on his knees with his hands inside the puppets raised up high. Audiences saw just the puppets, which ended at Jim's elbows. But what if he moved the wrong way by mistake? The viewers would see the top of his head.

Jim came up with a really smart idea. He put a small TV monitor on the floor in front of him. That way he could see what the camera was showing audiences. Today almost every puppeteer in television uses this technique.

Television required other changes in puppets. In live theater, puppets were made of wood or papier-mâché. Audiences were far away, so it didn't matter if the puppets' faces didn't move. But on TV, puppets were close up. Kukla and Ollie had cloth faces, so they had more expression. But they had wood or other hard material inside, so they appeared pretty stiff. Jim decided to make cloth puppets without stiff insides. With a twist of his fingers or wrist, he could make them smile or look surprised or angry. And he could make the puppets pretty fast and cheaply.

Jim found his mom's ragbag and took out an old, nubby, turquoise-green coat of hers. He cut the cloth into the shape he wanted and sewed it into a puppet. He added some cardboard and felt for the mouth. For eyes, he cut a ping-pong ball

in half. For eyeballs, he drew a black dot with a
line through it. Then he glued them on the
creature's face.

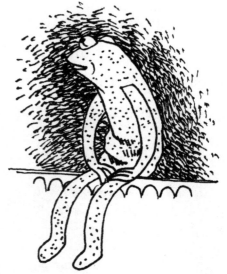

He didn't know it
then, but he had just
made one of the most
famous puppets
ever —Kermit the
Frog. Only this first
Kermit looked kind
of like a lizard. It was
lucky his mom's coat
was green, or Kermit might
never have become a frog at all!

Unlike most puppets, Jim's didn't look like
real people or animals. Instead, he created
oddball creatures that he called Muppets. He
chose the name because it was a cross between
"marionette" and "puppet" and because he liked
the sound. It was something new and different.

Jim loved music and used it in his Muppet shows from the very beginning. On early shows, the Muppets didn't speak. Instead, they sang popular songs. They did wild dances and funny skits. In one of the very first musical numbers, Sam and Kermit, in a blond wig, sang a love song

called "That Old Black Magic." Jim was always a little shy, but it was easy to show his silly side through his Muppets.

Sam and Friends was weird. It was fresh. It was a hit!

LONG BEFORE JIM'S KERMIT, THERE WAS ANOTHER FAMOUS ANIMAL ON TV—MICKEY MOUSE. WALT DISNEY IS THE MAN WHO CREATED HIM. IN 1928, WALT DISNEY'S COMPANY MADE *STEAMBOAT WILLIE,* ONE OF THE FIRST CARTOONS WITH SOUND, STARRING MICKEY MOUSE AND MINNIE MOUSE. DISNEY ALSO MADE THE FIRST FEATURE-LENGTH CARTOON MOVIE EVER IN 1937— *SNOW WHITE AND THE SEVEN DWARFS.*

GROWING UP, JIM HENSON REALLY LIKED WALT DISNEY'S ANIMATED MOVIES— *PINOCCHIO, FANTASIA,* (WHICH WERE MADE IN 1940), AND *DUMBO* (1941). WALT DISNEY CREATED OTHER CARTOON CHARACTERS LIKE DONALD DUCK, AND CAME UP WITH OTHER BIG IDEAS, LIKE THE DISNEYLAND AND WALT DISNEY WORLD RESORT THEME PARKS. WALT DISNEY WAS BORN IN 1901 AND DIED IN 1966. HE WON A WHOPPING TWENTY-SIX ACADEMY AWARDS DURING HIS LONG CAREER.

IN 2004, THE JIM HENSON COMPANY MADE A DEAL WITH THE WALT DISNEY COMPANY, TRANSFERRING RIGHTS OF THE "MUPPETS."

Chapter 3
More Muppeteers

When Jim was nineteen, something terrible happened. His brother, Paul, died in a car accident. Jim was very upset. His own life was going so well. It was hard to believe his brother's was over. After this awful event, Jim seemed more determined than ever to work hard and make the most out of his life.

Between his show and college classes, Jim had a lot to do. In puppet class, he met another student named Jane Nebel. She agreed to help work the puppets, paint sets, and sew costumes on *Sam and Friends*. She had a zany sense of humor. Jim and Jane made a good team.

In 1956, they took the Muppets on *The Tonight Show*, hosted by Steve Allen. It was a very popular show that aired at 11:30 at night. It was not a children's show. It was for grown-ups. But the Muppets were a hit. Jim operated Kermit. Jane operated Yorick, who gobbled up his own clothes and then tried to gobble up Kermit's leg, too! Muppets were always gobbling stuff up in the early days.

Soon after that, a company named Wilkins Coffee asked Jim to make TV commercials. Back then, most commercials were serious. But Jim had different ideas. He made funny commercials with the Muppets. And they were a hit. Jim made many more commercials for toothpaste, Chinese food, and other products. But commercials usually weren't as much fun for Jim as other work. They were all about selling, selling, selling.

With his first paychecks, Jim bought his parents a color TV and bought himself a T-bird convertible. Soon he had made enough to buy a used Rolls-Royce Silver Cloud, a very expensive

car. He drove it to his college graduation. All his life, he would collect flashy cars.

He and Jane had become good friends by now. They also became business partners. Muppets Inc. was born. Even so, Jim wasn't sure if being a puppeteer was what he wanted to do with his life. He still wanted to be an artist. He decided to put the Muppets away for a while and go to Europe. However, NBC wanted the Muppets to stay on. So Jane and a friend kept it going.

Jim traveled in Germany, Switzerland, Belgium, and England. He went to puppet shows in every country. In Europe, grown-ups were interested in puppets. Puppeteers were considered artists. In America, puppets were kid stuff. By the time he got home, Jim had decided he did want to be a puppeteer after all, but a puppeteer who created shows for people of all ages.

He also wanted to get married. Jim and Jane had fallen in love. They got married in May 1959. In the basement of their new home, Jim and Jane set up the first official Muppet workshop. *Sam and Friends* was still going strong and would last six years all together (1955-1961). It even won a local Emmy award. Their first daughter, Lisa, was born in 1960. In 1961, a daughter named Cheryl came along. Jim adored his kids—he was a kid at

heart himself. Once they had a family, Jane spent more time caring for the children at home. She did less performing, so Jim needed to find help with the Muppets.

At puppet festivals, he met other puppeteers. Jerry Juhl was the first to come work with him. Frank Oznowicz (Oz, for short) was still in high school, but Jim hoped he would come work for him someday. Jim also met Don Sahlin, who later became the head Muppet builder.

Jim and Don worked together very closely. For a new Muppet, Jim would think of an idea. He would doodle a quick sketch of his character on paper. In just a dozen or so scribbled lines, he could show the personality and look of the creature. Then he showed it to Don who made suggestions and did the actual building of the puppet. The first Muppet Don made was for a dog food commercial. It was a brown dog whose name was Rowlf.

All through his career, Jim had a knack for hiring talented people who worked well together. Even when businesspeople and lawyers joined his company much later, he made sure they got along with his creative crews.

Most people who worked with Jim liked him. He was so energetic that others caught his energy. He enjoyed and respected creative people. He didn't try to squash ideas just because they weren't his. People often stayed to work with him for years or even decades.

Chapter 4
The Big Time

In 1963, Jim and Jane decided to go where the work was—so the family moved to New York City. They'd become friends with Burr Tillstrom, the famous Kukla and Ollie puppeteer. They moved into the apartment building where Burr lived. Sometimes they hung out or had dinner together. Jim looked up to Burr and would go to him for advice.

Jim opened an office for Muppets Inc. on East 53rd Street. It wasn't a very big office. Don's puppet-building workshop was in one room. Jim and Jerry shared another room. Jim often wore jeans and flowered shirts and ties to work. Sometimes he wore a suede jacket and a leather hat.

It wasn't your typical office. Jim didn't like working at a desk: He spent most of his time flopped in a big, black chair, his long legs propped on a footstool. Yorick, his skull puppet, hung in his office window. Don built a long roadway made of Slinky toys and hollow plastic balls for seven mice that were office pets. The

road wound high in the air and along desks and cupboards. Imagine people's surprise when they came to visit!

With four people plus Muppets, the office was crowded. Then Frank Oz, who was nineteen at the time, joined their group as a puppeteer. Jerry stopped performing and did more writing, which he liked best.

The Muppets continued to appear in commercials. They also went on variety shows along with juggling acts and singing groups. In a skit on *The Jack Paar Show,* a popular nighttime talk show, Kermit begins nibbling on what looks like a worm. It turns out to be the long nose of a monster, who gobbles him up. Grown-ups thought this was hilarious.

But Kermit wasn't the first Muppet to become a big star. Rowlf the dog was. Rowlf appeared many times on a popular variety program— *The Jimmy Dean Show.*

Jimmy Dean and Rowlf did funny skits and sang duets. Audiences liked Rowlf's friendly face, floppy ears, and silly humor. The Muppet dog seemed almost real to audiences. Rowlf began getting thousands of fan letters—sometimes more than Jimmy Dean!

Jim Henson operated Rowlf's head and left hand, and did his gruff voice. Frank operated his right hand. Special sets had to be designed to hide Jim and Frank from the TV camera.

With every performance, Jim was learning. He saw that puppet comedy was different than people comedy. Puppets needed to *do* something funny, not just say something funny. He also realized that if the Muppets' mouths moved on every syllable of a word, it didn't look real. It was better if they moved only on the important beats.

Meanwhile, Jim and Jane's family was growing. Their first son, Brian, was born in 1963. John Henson was born two years later. The Hensons' family of six moved to a house in Greenwich, Connecticut, less than an hour from New York City.

They had a busy, fun life. Jim let his kids doodle colorful creatures on the walls of their house and always encouraged his children to be creative. The family wound up with lots of pets—eight cats, six rabbits, two dogs, guinea pigs, and a ferret.

At Halloween, he would carve fantastic, beastly jack-o-lanterns. The kids made their own costumes using scraps of puppet-making fabric, fur, and trimmings from the Muppet offices. They would make Easter eggs decorated with bugs and animals. One Christmas, Jim used bread dough to make hundreds of ornaments for the tree in the shapes of little monsters.

In 1966, the Muppets appeared on *The Ed Sullivan Show*. Famous acts like the Beatles and Elvis Presley went on this show. Jim and his Muppets had hit the big time.

Jim liked to have a lot of different projects going at once. He made a ten-minute movie starring himself called *Time Piece*. It is a

sometimes funny, sometimes disturbing film with almost no words and a jazz music background. It's about a man racing through different stages of life like love and work—and in one scene, he even paints an elephant! It was nominated for an Academy Award. He had ideas for other movies without Muppets, but those would have to wait. The Muppets were about to get a call from *Sesame Street*.

Chapter 5
Sesame Street

In 1969, a woman named Joan Ganz Cooney phoned Jim. She was working on a new kind of kids' TV show called *Sesame Street*. The idea was that it would make learning fun for very young children—a sort of preschool on TV.

Jim and Jane had four kids by now and would soon have their last child, Heather, in 1970. Jim liked the idea of a show that taught kids something and didn't talk down to them. It was something important to be a part of. Although he was busy, he decided to make time for *Sesame Street*.

Besides his small-sized Muppets, Jim was asked to create one special Muppet that would hang out on the street with the real actors. This Muppet would be way bigger than the people. But Jim wanted the Muppet to think like a kid, too. He hatched the idea of Big Bird.

Big Bird is an eight-foot-two, friendly, yellow bird, with a person inside. Jim, who was six foot three, planned to be Big Bird. But when he tried on the costume, someone told him that he didn't act birdlike. He agreed. A performer named Caroll Spinney took the job instead. Since he was shorter than Jim, he had to wear four-inch tall shoes to fit into the costume. Inside, there was a fan to help him stay cool and a TV monitor so he could see himself. Caroll Spinney has performed as Big Bird for over forty years.

The first show aired on November 10, 1969. *Sesame Street* was

more popular than anyone ever expected. Big
Bird wound up on the cover of *Time* magazine.
The Muppets were famous!

On *Sesame Street*, Kermit became a superstar.
By now he was all frog. He had a collar, frog feet,
and a pink tongue.

Some friends thought Jim was very much like
Kermit, easygoing and good at running things.

Jim thought Kermit was sometimes bolder than he was. Jim thought he was more like Rowlf. Jim always operated Kermit himself. He sang Kermit's song "Bein' Green," which became popular. It's about how being green may seem unexciting but it's really wonderful. Jim wanted all children to know they were wonderful, too.

Jim also played Ernie on *Sesame Street* and sang his hit song "Rubber Duckie." Frank Oz played Bert, Ernie's pal. Like Jim, Frank was shy about some things. For a while he was scared to do puppet voices. But on *Sesame Street*, he performed Bert, Grover, and Cookie Monster.

Jane and the Henson kids loved visiting the TV studio. Jim would take them out to lunch or for ice cream if he had time. Sometimes, the kids got to meet the guest star or even be in the show! When he was only six, Jim's son Brian was in a skit about how buildings get made. He and two other kids were shown digging in a sandbox.

Eventually, Jim moved his office and his workshop to East 69th Street in New York. The building had a spiral staircase and a huge hot air balloon sculpture his son John helped make out of wire, wood, and metal.

The Muppets were carefully stored in their

own drawers. There were also drawers full
of feathers, eyeballs, noses, foam faces, whiskers,
wigs, and fur. There were shelves with all
different sorts of cloth. There were long work
tables where new Muppets were built. If Kermit
wore out, a new Kermit was made.

Sometimes Jim would stop by to try out a new, partly-built Muppet. He liked to figure out problems—for instance, how to make a Muppet saxophone player's cheeks puff in and out. He was delighted if someone found a new kind of hair or eyeball that made a creature look more interesting.

When he liked something, he might call it "lovely." If he didn't like something, he wouldn't say so. He'd say, "Interesting." Or "hmm." And he'd offer suggestions to help. He always spoke softly, and moved his hands a lot to describe something.

Every week, Jim and his crew were given lists of topics for upcoming *Sesame Street* shows. It was their job to come up with fun, smart ways for the Muppets to teach things like letters, math, and shapes.

Jim still managed to find time to make TV specials like *The Great Santa Claus Switch*. He even made special Muppets for the late-night TV show, *Saturday Night Live*.

Jim had ideas for his own TV shows and movies that he wanted to create. But for now *Sesame Street* was keeping him awfully busy.

Chapter 6
The Muppet Show

One idea Jim kept thinking about was a weekly TV show with Muppets. He wanted it to be mainly for grown-ups. But people were used to seeing the Muppets on *Sesame Street* and thought they were just for kids.

In the early 1970s, there were only three national TV channels—ABC, NBC, and CBS. Jim pitched his idea to each one. They all said no. The only person interested was a producer in England. He wanted Jim's new show made there. Then later it could be sold to TV stations in America and around the world. Jim agreed.

Around this time, Jim changed the name of Muppets Inc. to Henson Associates (HA! for short). His company was making a lot of money

by now, so he bought a second house for his family in England. He would travel back and forth between London and New York to work on different projects.

The British producer wanted a different star to host each episode of Jim's new show. He thought that would appeal to grown-ups. It was hard to get guest stars. The first to say yes was South-African actress-dancer Juliet Prowse.

The Muppet Show was set in a theater supposedly owned by Muppets. Each week, they had to put on a new show. They joked around with the guest star. The star would be in a few skits. There were lots of funny problems and silly mistakes along the way. When the Muppets acted up, Kermit kept things under control.

It was almost like Kermit and the Muppets were copying what Jim and his crew did to create the TV episodes. In the middle of chaos, Jim and Kermit were both good problem-solvers, making sure things worked out okay. Frank Oz said that Jim hardly ever got angry. If Jim was annoyed, he didn't yell. He would just start flipping the pages of a script he was reading or shift in his chair.

In 1976, *The Muppet Show* premiered in the US. It was another hit for Jim! The audience for the show was mostly grown-ups, although plenty of kids watched, too. There was a big cast— sometimes hundreds of Muppets. That meant lots of puppeteers.

Once there weren't enough puppeteers on hand for a crowd scene so Jim asked visitors, janitors, and stagehands to help by holding one of the puppets.

Miss Piggy appeared on the first show and became an instant star. She was glamorous, with blue eyes and long, golden hair. She was pushy and knew what she wanted—to be famous and to marry Kermit. And she went after both of her goals, batting her eyelashes and giving karate chops. Frank Oz performed Miss Piggy. He thought that part of the reason she became so popular might have been because of the women's rights movement.

THE WOMEN'S RIGHTS MOVEMENT

WHEN JIM WAS GROWING UP, HIS MOM DIDN'T WORK OUTSIDE THE HOME. ONLY ABOUT 1/3 OF AMERICAN WOMEN DID IN THE 1950S. INSTEAD, THEY WERE ENCOURAGED TO GET MARRIED AND HAVE CHILDREN. WOMEN WHO DID WORK USUALLY WERE NURSES, TEACHERS, CLERKS, SECRETARIES, OR FACTORY WORKERS. THEY ALMOST ALWAYS EARNED LESS MONEY THAN MEN, EVEN AT THE VERY SAME JOBS! IF A WOMAN WANTED TO BE AN FBI AGENT OR AN AIRLINE PILOT, SHE COULD BE TOLD "NO" JUST BECAUSE SHE WAS A WOMAN.

IN THE 1960S, WOMEN BEGAN FORMING GROUPS, LIKE NOW—THE NATIONAL ORGANIZATION OF WOMEN—TO PUSH FOR EQUAL RIGHTS JUST AS AFRICAN AMERICANS HAD BEEN DOING SINCE THE MID-1950S. THE EQUAL PAY ACT OF 1963 AND THE CIVIL RIGHTS ACT OF 1964 WERE PASSED TO STOP UNFAIR TREATMENT OF PEOPLE BASED ON TRAITS THEY CAN'T CHANGE SUCH AS RACE, RELIGION, AND GENDER.

BY 1970, THE NUMBER OF WORKING WOMEN WAS UP TO 43 PERCENT. BY 1980, IT WAS OVER 50 PERCENT. AND BY 2000, ABOUT 60 PERCENT OF WOMEN HAD PART-TIME OR FULL-TIME CAREERS. OVER THE PAST FIFTY YEARS, WOMEN HAVE RISEN

TO POSITIONS OF GREAT IMPORTANCE SUCH AS
ASTRONAUTS, DOCTORS, SUPREME COURT
JUDGES, MEMBERS OF CONGRESS, NEWSPAPER
PUBLISHERS, AND HEADS OF BIG COMPANIES.

As *The Muppet Show* grew in popularity so did Miss Piggy.

Not all of the Muppets were stars. For crowd scenes, Whatnots were used. Whatnots were blank Muppet heads. Different eyes, noses, hair, and clothes are added to give them personalities.

Jim still performed Kermit and Rowlf, and did new Muppets like Dr. Teeth, the rock piano player, and Captain Link Hogthrob of the "Pigs in Space" skits.

Together, Jim and Frank did the Swedish Chef. Jim worked the chef's head with one arm and did his voice. Frank Oz's real hands were the chef's hands. They had a great time. Frank would do something wild and unexpected with the hands, and Jim would have to think fast. Once, Frank made the chef toss a fake chicken through a basketball hoop.

After the show was a hit, it was easy to get famous stars to come on. Before each show, Jim and the writers would meet with the star. Jim included Muppets in the meeting. This helped the star get comfortable talking to puppets.

Jim included his family in things when he could. The very first puppets his fifteen-year-old daughter Cheryl made were for the show—an artichoke, an asparagus, and a grapefruit. Her older sister, Lisa, made a tomato puppet. Their fruits and veggies sang a popular song from the 1920s: "Yes! We Have No Bananas."

Jim also included skits on subjects that were important to him. One was about a group of forest animals hiding from hunters with guns. A favorite episode of his starred Harry Belafonte, who sang the song "Turn the World Around" with the Muppets. It was about people of all races

learning to accept one another. By 1980, *The Muppet Show* was watched by 235 million people in more than one hundred countries. Kermit had hosted *The Tonight Show*. There was even a giant Kermit balloon in the famous Macy's Thanksgiving Day Parade.

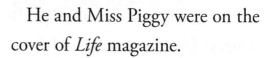

He and Miss Piggy were on the cover of *Life* magazine.

Then after five seasons, Jim decided to end the show.

Why? He wanted to stop while the Muppets were still on top.

Chapter 7
Muppets in the Movies

Because *The Muppet Show* was such a success, film companies were eager for Jim to make *The Muppet Movie*. Jim, of course, was eager to do it. He was ready for a new challenge.

In the first scene, Kermit plays a banjo and sings "Rainbow Connection." He's sitting on

a log in a swamp. Creating this scene with computer animation wasn't possible yet. So Jim found a way to perform this scene for real. The swamp log sat on top of a big, metal tank under a pool of water on a film set. Jim was inside the tank, with a small TV between his knees to watch Kermit. He stuck both hands up through rubber sleeves to work Kermit's head and banjo-strumming arm. A pump kept Jim supplied with air, and rescue divers were nearby in case of trouble. *The Muppet Movie* came out in 1979 and was a big hit!

The Great Muppet Caper came out in 1981. It did very well, too, though not as well as *The Muppet Movie*. Kermit, Fozzie Bear, and Gonzo are reporters on the case of a stolen diamond— a baseball diamond.

In one scene, Kermit, Miss Piggy, and a bunch of Muppets ride bicycles together. Audiences were amazed. How had Jim done this? It looked so

real. Remember, this was before computer animation. This is how it was done: The bike-riding Muppets were operated with strings from

above. Each bike was attached to another by
a rod connecting the wheels. Up ahead, riders on
two tricycles pulled the bikes on long strings.
Jim's son Brian rode one of the trikes.

TWO MAIN KINDS OF MUPPETS

A HAND-AND-ROD MUPPET: A PUPPETEER'S RIGHT HAND GOES UP THE MUPPET'S BODY TO ITS HEAD, LIKE PUTTING ON A GLOVE. LONG, THIN RODS ARE ATTACHED TO THE MUPPET'S HANDS. THE PUPPETEER HOLDS THE ENDS OF BOTH RODS IN ONE HAND TO MAKE THE MUPPET DO SIMPLE THINGS LIKE CLAP. IF THE MUPPET NEEDS TO DO MORE COMPLICATED MOVEMENTS, ANOTHER PUPPETEER HELPS. KERMIT THE FROG IS A HAND-AND-ROD MUPPET.

A LIVE-HAND MUPPET: TWO PUPPETEERS ARE
NEEDED TO OPERATE THIS KIND OF PUPPET. ONE
SLIPS HIS RIGHT HAND INTO THE HEAD AND HIS
LEFT HAND INTO THE PUPPET'S LEFT HAND. THE
OTHER PUPPETEER SLIPS HER HAND INSIDE
THE MUPPET'S RIGHT HAND. ERNIE IS A LIVE-HAND
MUPPET.

As the Muppets did more complicated things, more staff was needed. Now and then, Jim held puppeteer tryouts. Not everyone was right for the Muppets. The work was fun. But it was hard, too.

People's arms got tired and sore from holding heavy puppets for a long time. Puppeteers had to work in uncomfortable positions. If a bunch of Muppets ran around together, the performers had to run around together underneath them. Jim thought that with enough practice, the puppet almost becomes part of the puppeteer. But it took a year or longer for a puppeteer to become good enough to work a main Muppet.

Chapter 8
A Different Kind of Movie

Now that the Muppets were superstars, Jim was super busy. In the 1980s, he often had to travel. It was exciting—he rode a camel in Egypt, he went hot air ballooning in France.

Jim still tried to find time to be with his family. By now, Lisa and Cheryl had graduated from college. Brian, John, and Heather were teenagers. His kids admired him, liked hanging out with him, and often worked with him. Jim thought they had good, funny ideas. He listened to their advice and trusted them. They played tennis, went snow skiing, and sailed together. They also enjoyed simple things like going on walks and flying kites.

Jim was a modest, private person. He enjoyed just sitting alone in a garden thinking. He was rich. He had several homes and fancy cars, including a Kermit-green Lotus. Every year he held a lavish costume party to thank his employees. He always wore a tuxedo and a super-fancy mask.

But fame and money were never the most important things to Jim. He created The Jim

Henson Foundation to get people interested in puppetry. He made commercials about recycling and helping the environment.

Times were changing. As always, Jim was ready to push the limits of what puppets could do. He was interested in animatronics. This was a new way of moving puppets using computers and radio controls. He helped the creators of *Star Wars* to create the Yoda puppet. Frank Oz did Yoda's voice.

Jim used animatronics in *The Dark Crystal*. It was his first fantasy movie. He was so excited about animatronics that he decided not to use any real people in the movie. Instead, he would use only puppets.

His daughter Cheryl helped him with the plot. In the story, the evil Skeksis have taken control of the planet Thra. Gentle creatures called Mystics are now under their thumb. To save the planet, two fairylike Gelflings join forces.

A famous fantasy illustrator named Brian Froud came up with the look of the characters in *The Dark Crystal*. The puppets were full-figured. That means they had bodies with arms and legs. They were radio-controlled or hand-operated by puppeteers. For the larger characters, human actors wore costumes. It was exhausting work. Some costumes were so heavy that the actors had to be hung up on the wall—costume and all— for short rest breaks.

A lot of space was needed to create all the sets and characters. So Jim bought an old post office building across the street from his house in London. It had high ceilings and big open spaces. It became known as The Creature Shop.

Many people went to see *The Dark Crystal* when it was released in 1982. Jim had really enjoyed making it. He was proud that he'd tried something new.

But some audiences were confused. Where

were the Muppets? They weren't sure if it was for grown-ups or kids. *The Dark Crystal* was nowhere near as popular as Steven Spielberg's *E.T.: The Extra-Terrestrial* which came out the same year. Jim was disappointed, but he knew he'd done good work . . . besides, he was already on to the next new project.

Chapter 9
Always Something New

Jim's next TV show, *Fraggle Rock,* was meant to encourage world peace. It debuted in 1983 and it included three kinds of puppets. The Fraggles were medium-sized hand Muppets. The Doozers were little remote-controlled creatures. The Gorgs were big puppets with actors inside. These creatures didn't like one another, but they needed one another. So they had to learn to cooperate. Jim was trying to show how different groups can learn to get along.

In 1984, *Jim Henson's Muppet Babies* cartoon show began airing on Saturday mornings. The idea came from a scene in his third Muppet movie, *The Muppets Take Manhattan,* which had shown the Muppets as babies.

Jim also made a second fantasy film called *Labyrinth.* His daughters Lisa and Cheryl helped with some of the plot ideas. Cheryl and Jim's son Brian operated some of the puppets.

In *Labyrinth*, a girl must make her way through a labyrinth—which is another word for a maze—to rescue her baby brother from a goblin. Jim decided it had been a mistake not to use some real actors along with the puppets in *The Dark Crystal*. This time, he did things differently. Rock star David Bowie played the Goblin King.

Labyrinth had more humor and songs, too. Still, audiences didn't like it as much as the Muppet movies. This was a great disappointment for Jim.

The same year *Labyrinth* premiered, he and Jane separated. They had grown apart over the

years, probably partly because work had often kept Jim away from home. They never divorced, and the Hensons stayed a close family. In fact, some of the Henson kids were grown now and working full-time for the company. Still, it was a difficult time for Jim, Jane, and their kids.

Chapter 10
Good-bye Too Soon

Jim Henson never ran out of ideas. He was always excited to be starting something new. But running the business of the Muppets took up a lot of his time.

In 1989, he decided to sell some of the Muppet characters to the Walt Disney Company. He thought the Disney people would take good care of the Muppets' future. But before the deal went through, something terrible happened.

It began when Jim got a cold. At least that was

what he thought it was. He figured the cold would go away. Jim hardly ever got sick. He didn't smoke and was careful to eat well. When he did get sick, he never liked making a fuss about it.

The following week, Jim decided to visit his dad in North Carolina. He still felt sick and was having trouble sleeping. Back in New York, he

got worse. Jane helped take care of him. When he didn't come to work one day, his crew knew Jim's illness must be serious. He hardly ever took time off. At last, Jim went to the hospital. He had pneumonia, a very dangerous kind. When the crew found out, everyone began calling everyone. Friends and family came to the hospital as doctors worked to save Jim's life. It was a horrible, confusing time.

On May 16, 1990, Jim died. His death surprised and saddened the world. People could hardly believe he was gone. Many children sent hand-drawn sympathy cards to honor Jim. Disney sent a big card with a picture of Mickey Mouse hugging a sad Kermit.

Memorial services were held in his honor in New York and in London. The one in New York was in a beautiful stone cathedral called St. John the Divine. Thousands of people went. The cathedral filled up. More people kept coming and

some even stood outside. They just wanted to be there to celebrate the life of Jim Henson. Jim hadn't expected to die at age fifty-three. But he had written down what he would like at such a memorial service. He'd hoped there would be music and that people would tell nice stories about their time with him.

That's what happened. A Dixieland jazz band played "When the Saints Go Marching In." Big Bird came and sang Kermit's famous song, "Bein' Green." It was a song Jim Henson had always performed. In the crowd, there were kids holding toy Ernies, Berts, and Big Birds. Friends, family, and coworkers stood and told stories about fun times with Jim. Frank Oz spoke of Jim's generosity and how great it was to hear him laugh. Speaking to the crowd, Jane Henson said, "I hope that you'll take whatever he's given you and let it help you to enjoy life to the fullest, because he always did."

His son Brian read aloud part of a letter Jim

had written for his children. It said: "Please watch out for each other and love and forgive everybody. It's a good life, enjoy it."

His daughter Cheryl read other words of her father: "When I was young, my ambition was to be one of the people who makes a difference in this world. My hope still is to leave this world a little bit better than it was when I got here."

To this day, the Muppets are beloved around the world. So is Jim Henson.

JIM'S FAMILY

JIM'S FIVE CHILDREN ARE GROWN-UP NOW. TOGETHER, THEY OWN AND RUN THE JIM HENSON COMPANY. IT CREATES THE PUPPETS THAT APPEAR ON *SESAME STREET*. (IN 2001, THE RIGHTS TO THE ORIGINAL *SESAME STREET* CHARACTERS CREATED BY THE JIM HENSON COMPANY WERE SOLD TO SESAME WORKSHOP.)

ALL OF JIM HENSON'S CHILDREN ARE CREATIVE, LIKE THEIR FATHER. THIS IS JUST SOME OF WHAT THEY'VE DONE:

LISA, JIM'S OLDEST DAUGHTER, INSPIRED *THE STORYTELLER* SERIES. SHE IS THE CO-CEO OF THE COMPANY. SHE WAS THE PRESIDENT OF COLUMBIA PICTURES FOR TWO YEARS AND WORKED AT WARNER BROS. FOR TEN YEARS DURING THE TIME THE MOVIE *BATMAN* WAS MADE.

CHERYL WAS IN CHARGE OF THE HENSON INTERNATIONAL FESTIVAL OF PUPPET THEATER FOR EIGHT YEARS AND HELPED BRING PUPPETEERS FROM AROUND THE WORLD TO NEW YORK CITY. BEFORE THAT, SHE HELPED WITH *THE MUPPET SHOW*, *THE DARK CRYSTAL*, AND *LABYRINTH*.

BRIAN WAS THE PRESIDENT OF THE COMPANY FOR A WHILE AFTER JIM DIED. HE IS NOW CO-CEO WITH LISA. OVER THE YEARS, HE HAS BEEN A PUPPET-MAKER, A PUPPETEER, A WRITER, AND HAS DIRECTED AND PRODUCED TV SHOWS AND FILMS.

JOHN IS AN ARTIST AND SCULPTOR, WHO HAS MADE FILMS AND HAS PERFORMED THE MUPPET SWEETUMS.

HEATHER, JIM'S YOUNGEST CHILD, KEEPS BUSY WITH THE COMPANY, THE JIM HENSON FOUNDATION, AND THE JIM HENSON LEGACY. SHE HELPS PROMOTE PUPPETRY, AND WORKS ON TV, FILM, AND THEATER PROJECTS.

JANE HENSON AND JIM'S FAMILY AND FRIENDS ESTABLISHED THE JIM HENSON LEGACY IN 1993. THIS PROJECT COLLECTS AND PROTECTS EVERYTHING THEY CAN FIND ABOUT JIM'S LIFE AND WORK, INCLUDING HIS DRAWINGS AND OLD PUPPETS. *JIM HENSON'S FANTASTIC WORLD* IS AN EXHIBIT THEY CREATED WITH THE SMITHSONIAN INSTITUTION. IT HAS TRAVELED TO CITIES LIKE SEATTLE AND ORLANDO. IN WASHINGTON, D.C., OVER 360,000 PEOPLE TOURED IT!

TIMELINE OF
JIM HENSON'S LIFE

1936 —— Jim is born in Greenville, Mississippi

1948 —— The Henson family moves to Hyattsville, Maryland

1954 —— Jim enters the University of Maryland and meets Jane Nebe⟨

1955 —— *Sam and Friends* begins on TV;
Jim's brother, Paul, dies in a car accident

1956 —— The Muppets appear on *The Tonight Show*

1957 —— Jim makes his first TV commercial

1958 —— Jim travels to Europe

1959 —— Jim and Jane Nebel marry

1960 —— Jim graduates from college
The Hensons' first child, Lisa, is born

1961 —— Daughter Cheryl is born

1963 —— The Hensons move to New York City;
Son Brian is born

1965 —— Son John is born

1966 —— The Muppets go on *The Ed Sullivan Show*

1969 —— *Sesame Street* premieres on TV

1970 —— Daughter Heather is born

1976 —— *The Muppet Show* premieres on TV

1982 —— *The Dark Crystal* opens in theaters

1990 —— Jim dies on May 16

1991 —— A star for Jim Henson is placed
on the Hollywood Walk of Fame

TIMELINE OF THE WORLD

Franklin D. Roosevelt wins the presidential election for the second time — **1936**

Television officially begins broadcasting in the US; World War II begins — **1939**

World War II ends — **1945**

The first regularly-scheduled shows begin airing on TV — **1947**

The first color television set is available — **1954**

Disneyland opens in Anaheim, California; Rosa Parks is arrested in Alabama for refusing to give up her bus seat — **1955**

Martin Luther King Jr. gives his "I have a dream" speech in Washington, D.C.; President John F. Kennedy is assassinated — **1963**

The Beatles, a British rock group, comes to the US — **1964**

Nearly 100,000 people gather in Washington, D.C., to protest the Vietnam War. — **1967**

Astronaut Neil Armstrong walks on the moon; Woodstock music festival takes place in upstate New York — **1969**

Shirley Chisholm is the first African-American woman to run for US president — **1972**

President Richard Nixon resigns — **1974**

US celebrates its 200th birthday — **1976**

The Challenger explodes seventy-three seconds after takeoff, killing all seven astronauts — **1986**

The Berlin Wall falls — **1989**

BIBLIOGRAPHY

Bacon, Matt. **No Strings Attached: The Inside Story of Jim Henson's Creature Shop.** Macmillan, New York, 1997.

*Durrett, Deanne. **Inventors and Creators—Jim Henson.** KidHaven Press, The Gale Group, San Diego, 2002.

*Durrett, Deanne. **The Importance of Jim Henson.** Lucent Books, San Diego, 1994.

Finch, Christopher. **Jim Henson: The Works— The Art, the Magic, the Imagination.** Random House, New York, 1993.

*Gikow, Louise. **Meet Jim Henson.** Random House, New York, 1993.

*Gourse, Leslie. **Jim Henson: Young Puppeteer.** Aladdin Paperbacks, New York, 2000.

*Inches, Allison. **Jim Henson's Designs and Doodles.** H. N. Abrams, New York, 2001.

*Parish, James Robert. **Jim Henson: Puppeteer and Filmmaker.** Ferguson, Infobase Publishing, New York, 2006.

*St. Pierre, Stephanie. **The Story of Jim Henson: Creator of the Muppets.** Gareth Stevens Publishing, Milwaukee, 1997.

*Woods, Geraldine. **Jim Henson: From Puppets to Muppets.** Dillon Press, Minneapolis, 1987.

*Books for young readers

How to Make a Puppet

If you want to try making a puppet, here are some books that may help you.

- **Make Your Own Puppets & Puppet Theaters** by Carolyn Carreiro

- **101 Hand Puppets: A Beginner's Guide to Puppeteering** by Richard Cummings

- **The Usborne Book of Puppets** by Ken Haines and Gill Harvey

- **The Muppets Make Puppets!** by Cheryl Henson and the Muppet Workshop

- **Puppet Mania!** by John Kennedy

- **The Complete Book of Puppetry** by George Latshaw

- **Hand Puppets: How to Make and Use Them** by Laura Ross